STREAMS OF SONLIGHT

Andrew McConnaughie

Copyright © 2004 by Andrew McConnaughie

Streams Of Sonlight
by Andrew McConnaughie

Printed in the United States of America

ISBN 1-594672-94-6

All rights reserved solely by the author. The author guarantees all contents are original and do not infringe upon the legal rights of any other person or work. No part of this book may be reproduced or transmitted in any form or by any means—electronic, mechanical, photocopy, recording or information storage and retrieval system—except for brief quotations in printed reviews—without the prior, written permission of the author. The views expressed in this book are not necessarily those of the publisher.

Unless otherwise indicated, Bible quotations are taken from the New King James Version. Copyright © 1988 by Thomas Nelson, Inc.

www.xulonpress.com

DEDICATIONS

To my wife, whose love, friendship and faithfulness mean more than words can express.
-- My son, Steve, 'daughter' Yvonne, and granddaughters, Leah, Lori and Lisa.
-- My daughter, Ruth, 'son' Mark, grandson Joshua and granddaughter Holly.

-- In memory of my parents: Andrew and Mary McConnaughie: and mother and father-in-law, Robert and Lorna Johnson, whose godly example was a perpetual source of encouragement.

ACKNOWLEDGEMENTS

To my wife, Pat, whose unending patience and determination never cease to amaze me. Without her unstinting support this work would not be in print.
-- Lori, who provided the initial design for the book cover and assisted with typing.
-- Lisa, who also aided with her typing skills.
-- Mark, with his computer expertise rescued us numerous times from 'impending disaster.'
-- The many friends whose counsel and encouragement helped make 'Streams of Sonlight' possible.

Streams Of Sonlight

CONTENTS

Water Of Life	9
New Wine	10
Wake-Up Call	12
Streams Of Sonlight	14
A New Dimension	16
A Gentle Breeze	18
Hope	20
Catch The Vision	22
Light For The Lost	24
Essential Faith	26
The First Advent	28
Harvesters	30
Blessed	32
Shouts Of Joy	34
A New Anointing	36
God's Supremacy	38
Spiritual Circumcision	40
Our Father	42
Released	44
Weapons Of Warfare	46
Rejoice	48
The Name Of Jesus	50
Song Of Encouragement	52
The Deluge Promise	54
Arise My Love	56
To Be Sure	60
Faith Triumphs	62
Praise And Worship	64
My Kingdom	66
Rivers Of Renewal	68
The Lord Reigns	70
Fear Not	72

CONTENTS

Prepare For Battle	74
Help	76
Who Is He?	78
Old Or New	80
Everlasting	82
Covenant Blessing	84
Then Came The Morning	86
Revival Blessing	88
Man Of Sorrows	90
My Presence	92
Behold!	94
Divine Attachment	96
In The Midst	98
I Will Return	100
Gifts Anyone?	102
The Things I Have Done	104
The Power Of The Blood	106
Rediscover	108
All Rise	110
Carried Away	112
Power In Praise	114
Promises	116
Day Of Deliverance	118
This Mountain	120
The River Is Flowing	122
Yes, Lord	124
My House	126
Spiritual Warfare	128
Homecoming	132
Worthy Is The Lamb	134
Your King Comes	136
I Am	138

Streams Of Sonlight

WATER OF LIFE

Ho! Everyone who thirsts, come to the waters, come and drink of the Water of Life freely.
**Come My children
Come without waiting
Come, for the rivers are deep and the waters are plentiful**
Through My prophet Isaiah, I have promised to pour water on him who is thirsty and floods on the dry ground. As your sovereign Lord, I know this is the desire of your heart.
You are hungry and thirsty, ready and waiting; therefore, I have made provision for all your need. Do not be discouraged or disheartened; let your soul delight itself in My abundance.
Right now...
**My rivers are overflowing
My everlasting doors are lifted high**

There is more than enough for everyone. My people! Incline your ear to Me. Adhere to My counsel and direction and I will cause the windows of Heaven to be opened wide and showers of refreshing to be poured out upon you, even in this latter day, for you have made Me your God and King and I am glorified in you.

Isaiah 55:1   Isaiah 35:6-7   Malachi 3:10

PERSONAL RESOLVE

_____
_____

NEW WINE

My people

I speak words of encouragement…
      To the weak…**strength and grace**
     To the poor…**provision and bountifulness**
       To the fearful…**peace and calm**
To those who suffer loss and misfortune I extend to you…
        Beauty for ashes
     The oil of joy for mourning
The garment of praise for the spirit of heaviness

I want you to lean on Me, cast all your care upon Me, know My peace which passes all understanding, prosper and have good success. Be it known to you that I am a good God; I desire only what is best for you. Every good and perfect gift comes from Me, and in Me there is no variableness or shadow of turning.

I promise…
If you continue to walk in My precepts and be obedient to My voice…
   Your kindred and you shall excel in blessing
     Your barns will be filled with plenty
  Your grape vessels will overflow with New Wine
My prophet Joel, writes…
"It shall come to pass in the last days that the mountains shall drip with **New Wine**…and you shall know that I am the Lord."
Come to Me with increased faith and open hands

and I will bless according to your need.
I am Jehovah Jireh

> Giving does not impoverish Me
> Withholding does not enrich Me

Reach out now, believe and receive.

Joel 3:18   *Acts 2:17*   *Ezekiel 11:19*

PERSONAL RESPONSE

_____
_____
_____

WAKE-UP CALL

My children

Join with Me as I proclaim My wake-up call today…Blow the trumpet in Zion! Sound the alarm in My holy mountain!

Call the people together and come before Me in true repentance, I am gracious and merciful, slow to anger and swift to forgive. I will not give your promised inheritance to the unrighteous. You shall eat the good of the land.

Your wilderness shall rejoice
Your desert places will blossom
Your barren and thirsty land shall burst forth
with springs of living water

Therefore, cleanse and sanctify yourselves and I will do wonders among you. Let My servants weep between the porch and the altar. The time has come for all who name My name to turn to Me with fasting, weeping and mourning. Rend your hearts and not your garments, peradventure the Lord may turn away His wrath and leave behind Him a blessing or some new thing.

Call upon Me and I will answer you and show you great and mighty things which you have not yet known. I will send you rain, even the latter rain and you shall experience times of refreshing issuing forth from My presence.
In that day I will **wake up** your mighty men and

drive away all your enemies. I will restore to you the years that the locusts have eaten.

My people will again rejoice and be glad
They shall dance the dance of the righteous
Many shall see it and fear and put their trust in the Lord

Church! The Lord your God dwells in Zion...
Let all the ransomed praise My name...**My name is as ointment poured forth,** going out over all the land.

Joel 2 *Jeremiah 33:3* *Psalm 98:4-8*

PERSONAL PRAISE

_____
_____
_____

STREAMS OF SONLIGHT

I have spoken to you the prophetic word, delivered by prophets, priests and kings, but in these last days I have spoken to you through My beloved Son.

I have revealed Him as…
>> **Your Savior**
>> **Your Shelter**
>> **Your Song**

I desire you to…
> **Know His saving, sanctifying and transforming love**
> **Experience the richness of His grace and supremacy of His might**
> **Recognize the God of Jeshurun, who rides the heavens to help and places His everlasting arms around you**

You are My Blood-bought, Blood-washed, Heaven-born and Heaven-bound people. I want you to light up the world in which you live. My Son, Jesus, is and always has been the Light of the world. He is the Daystar and Dayspring, and continually beams forth streams of light into your world of darkness. He can do no other, for in Him is no darkness at all.

He is the Light who lights up the hearts of all men. Even the New Jerusalem has no need of the sun or moon, for
>> **Jesus the Lamb is the Light**

I yearn for streams of Sonlight to radiate from every

sector of My handiwork. I implore you and all of creation to emanate My glory.

The trees clap their hands
The lilies dance before Me
The seas roar and all the hills are joyful together

Sing to Me with joyfulness
Shout aloud with gladness
Dance freely with cheerfulness

Offer to Me thanksgiving and praise, with the sound of trumpets, timbrels and stringed instruments. You who have breath, exalt My name.

2 Peter 1:19   *Revelation 21:23*   *Psalm 150*

PERSONAL PRAISE

_____
_____
_____

A NEW DIMENSION

My chosen generation

Because you have made Me your strength, your refuge and your habitation, all My resources are yours. Behold! I will cast My mantle upon you and impart the...
> **Spirit of wisdom**
> **Spirit of understanding**
> **Spirit of counsel and knowledge**

A new awareness of My presence will be evident. A spirit of faith and expectancy will be released and recognized among you. You will launch out into new areas of love, faith and the miraculous. Divine fire will be prevalent in all your activities.

You will be impelled to cry out...
> **"This is our God, this is our King!**
> We have sought His face.
> We have interceded and believed.
> Our hearts have been heavy.
> Our pillows have been wet with tears.

Now our day of visitation has come. Our time of jubilation has arrived. Our God again, has made Himself known. He has come with renewed power and blessing, and with **a new dimension** of spiritual light and life. We have not seen it in this fashion before.

We will arise and...

Give Him praise and glory
Lift Him up above all others
Declare His name in the midst of the people

With joy and gladness we welcome and confess…
His mercy
His grace
His power

He has intervened and we will invest in Him."

Psalm 91:9   *Isaiah 43:19*   *Exodus 14:13*

PERSONAL RESPONSE

_____
_____
_____

A GENTLE BREEZE

Awake! Awake! O daughter of Zion

Put on your garment of praise.
Break forth into singing...Clap your hands and shout for joy, your day of emancipation has come. I will send a soft, **gentle breeze of My Spirit** upon you. Doors will open to you as you step out into a brand new day, causing your future to be better than the past has ever been...

Fetters will be broken
Burdens lifted
Obstacles removed
Opportunities given

I announce to you this day that oppression, fear and terror shall not come near your dwelling place. Your mountains are going to melt like wax before the mid-day sun. Your Red Seas are going to part, to the left and to the right. Miracles will be a regular occurrence in your midst.

I will take you out of the old paths and place you in the new. I will make you fruitful in every good work and increase you daily with benefits.

I have seen your labor of love to My people at home and overseas. Therefore, I choose to bless you and cause My mercies to descend upon you...**new every morning**.

I will be your...

**Sword and shield
Shelter and strength
Song and salvation
Sure source of ample supply**

Trust Me, My children, cast every care upon Me. Lean not to your own understanding. In all your ways acknowledge Me and I will direct your paths. I will order your steps.
I am the One who loves you always,
Jesus

Isaiah 61:3   Isaiah 52:12   Proverbs 3:5-6

PERSONAL COMMITMENT

_____
_____
_____

HOPE

My prophet Habakkuk cried out in a dire situation...
> "Though the fig tree may not blossom
> Though there be no fruit on the vine
> No corn in the field
> No flock in the sheep fold
> No herd in the stalls,
> **Yet, I will rejoice in the Lord...I will joy in the God of my salvation."**

My children...
Though your way may be rough and steep, and dark clouds hover over you...do not be alarmed, I am your sovereign Lord. When opposing circumstances prevail upon you, My love and compassion encircle you. You may be hard-pressed on every side, confused, despondent or feeling abandoned. You may sense heaviness upon you and your strength daily wasting away.

Do not lose heart; **hope in Me.** The day is fast approaching when you will rise up to praise and magnify My holy name. Lazarus, My servant, died and was laid in a tomb.
Heavy hearts were hurting, and many tears were shed. When I heard, I came, I wept and cried out, "Lazarus, come forth!" He who was dead came walking out of the tomb. Hope was reawakened in the hearts of Mary and Martha.

Only believe, and you shall see My glory.

I have redeemed you, I have called you by your name...
You are Mine
You are twice Mine...
Mine by right of creation
Mine by right of redemption

Trust Me, I am your...
>Rock and refuge
>Shelter in the time of storm

1 Peter 1:3 *Psalm 42:5* *Job 13:15*

PERSONAL ASSURANCE

_____
_____
_____

CATCH THE VISION

Children of Zion

Listen to My voice...
Because you have honored Me and not shunned to own My name, I will bless and honor you.

You have not failed to put on...
The breastplate of righteousness
The helmet of salvation
The garment of praise and thanksgiving

You shall be called...
The trees of righteousness
The planting of the Lord
You shall be as a well-watered garden, your increase going out over the wall.

Since you have walked humbly before Me and blessed those around you in their time of need, I will bless you one hundredfold and impart to you an increased desire to see My kingdom extended.
The time has come for you to go and tell what good things I have done for you.

Catch the vision...Do not tarry...
Run and share it with the nations
Stand on your high places and shout aloud that this is My dwelling place. There is bread in the house, sufficient for everyone.

Declare to the people that I am in My holy

mountain and if they seek Me they shall find Me, when they search for Me with all their hearts.

Arise! Shine! Your light has come; My glory is risen upon you. When unbelievers behold this glory, they will grasp your sleeve and say,
> "**Let us go with you, for we have heard that God is with you.**"

Genesis 49:22   Isaiah 60:1   Zechariah 8:23

PERSONAL COMMISSION

_____
_____
_____

LIGHT FOR THE LOST

Who is a God like Me, pardoning all iniquity?
I will remove your transgressions from you.

Repent and be converted that your sins may be blotted out and times of refreshing will come from My presence.

Receive My free gift of salvation and begin your new life today.

Rejoice! Your sins are now forgiven; you are a new creation in Me, your Lord and Savior. A place is prepared for you in Heaven. Be confident, you are a newborn child of the kingdom.

Endeavor to…
Seek first My kingdom
Lead others to salvation
Be filled with the Holy Spirit

Be alert! The devil is real…he may be defeated, but he is not dead. He is your adversary.
My word makes known he…
Goes about seeking whom he may devour
Tempts you to doubt your salvation
Attempts to make you ashamed of the gospel
Lures you into believing that should you sin, all hope of restoration in Me is gone

This is part of the enemy's strategy and contrary to My precepts and principles. If you confess your sin and turn from it, I will forgive you freely, adding strength to your experience, enabling you to overcome.

Be encouraged...
> **I formed you in the womb**
> **I focused My love upon you**
> **I found you and brought you to Myself**

I have given My angels charge over you to keep you in all your ways.

Micah 7:18   *Luke 10:20*   *1 John 1:7-10*

PERSONAL DECISION

_____
_____
_____

ESSENTIAL FAITH

Sing! O daughter of Zion. **Shout!** O people of Israel. **Be glad!** O church of the first-born. I am your God and I joy over you.

> **I cast My mantle of love over you**
> **I cause My Spirit to flow down over you**
> **I cease not to draw you closer and lift you higher**

It is here where...
> Heaven and earth meet and greet one another
> The devil is defeated
> The impossible becomes possible
> I bless you and supply your needs

When I walked on the earth in the flesh, I performed miracles...I have not changed with the years.
I can still turn...
> **Water into wine**
> **Sinners into saints**
> **Sorrow into joy**
> **I can still feed the multitude and have baskets full left over**

Faith is diminishing and with little faith you limit Me. As your effectual and loving Lord I urge you to catch a fresh glimpse of My passion, power and program for the world today. Let go of unbelief and increase your faith, you will then have authority and boldness to say to your mountain, "Be removed and be cast into the sea." And it shall be so.

My people, I yearn that you enjoy all the good things I have pledged. It is mandatory therefore, that

you be enlightened and motivated by My word. All things are possible to those who believe.
According to your faith, be it unto you

Zephaniah 3:17   Hebrews 13:8   Matthew 21:21

PERSONAL RESOLVE

_____
_____
_____

THE FIRST ADVENT

To everything there is a season and a time for every purpose under Heaven. I have made all things beautiful in their time. The first advent is a time to celebrate and a time to contemplate meaningful truths.

Envisage the starlit sky on that night when the angel hovered over the shepherds on the hillside, delivered the message of great joy and peace and sang with a host, their song of jubilation...
"Glory to God in the highest and on earth peace, goodwill toward men.
Jesus the Savior is born."

Marvel at the awesomeness of the day when **He will return** and receive you to Himself.
My word teaches...
He is coming in person
He is coming in power
Not as the lowly Jesus, riding on a donkey but as the **Mighty Conqueror,** riding on a white horse with a two-edged sword in His hand.
When He descends, every eye shall see Him and every tongue confess that He is Christ the Lord.

Ponder the truths He taught, the mercy He showed and the miracles He performed.

Consider what He has done for all men everywhere.
He has made it possible for every...

Sinner to be saved by His matchless love and grace
Child of the kingdom to live a life pleasing to Him
and rule and reign with Him forever

Give thanks for...
My unspeakable gift
I so loved the world, I gave My only Son, that whoever believes in Him, should not perish but have everlasting life.

Ecclesiastes 3:1   *Luke 2:13-14*   *John 3:16*

PERSONAL THANKSGIVING

_____
_____
_____

HARVESTERS

My children, you are...
> **The branch of My planting**
> **The work of My hands**
> **My pleasure throughout the ages**

You are a holy nation, a chosen generation, and I have ordained you to make known My name among the people.
I call on you to...
> **Stand up**
> **Cry aloud**
> **Spare nothing**
> **Tell the nations that I am on My throne**

> My ear is not heavy that it cannot hear
> My hand is not shortened that it cannot save
> My unlimited love knows no boundaries

I change and transform those who place their trust in Me. This is the day of opportunity. This is the hour for the redeemed of the Lord to say so. Let it be known, they who turn many to righteousness shall shine as the stars forever.

> **You are My witnesses and ambassadors**

You are workers together with Me in My vineyard. Go out, for the fields are white unto harvest and the laborers are few. I urge you, lay aside every obstruction...
Put in the sickle...
> **Today is the day of salvation**

Begin to rejoice; harvest time has come. You will go out weeping, bearing precious seed and doubtless come again rejoicing, bringing your sheaves with you.

The harvest is plentiful, prepare for a great ingathering

1 Peter 2:9 *Psalm 126:5-6* *John 4:35*

RESPONSE TO HARVEST

_____
_____
_____

BLESSED

Blessed is the man who walks not in the counsel of the ungodly, nor stands in the path of the unrighteous. His delight shall be in the law of the Lord. He shall be like a tree planted by the rivers of water. He shall bring forth fruit in every season and whatever he does will prosper.

My beloved, I want **you** to be…
> **Blessed**
> **Fruitful**
> **Prosperous**
> **Lenders and not borrowers**

All this was part of My covenant with Israel and can be yours today. If you will meditate on My word, hide it in your heart and make it the rule of your life, **you will be blessed.**

There is no want to those who fear Me. The young lions may lack and suffer hunger, but those who seek Me shall not lack any good thing.

Be encouraged My children, you are…
> **My purchased possession**
> **My workmanship**
> **My beloved**

Lift up your heads, your hands and your hearts. Run the race with patience. Do not be weary in well doing, for in due season you shall reap if you faint not.
> **I am your heavenly Father**

You are blessed; blessed with every spiritual blessing in heavenly places…according to My good pleasure.

Psalm 1   *Deuteronomy 28:1-14*   *Eph 2:10*

PERSONAL RESPONSE

_____
_____
_____

SHOUTS OF JOY

Children of the Vine

My servant Job walked the dark valley of pain and the road of loss and disheartenment, but through it all he cried out, "Even though my God should slay me, yet will I trust in Him...I know that my redeemer lives." Then I filled his mouth with laughter and his tongue with shouts of joy.

My people, look to Me! I am the Lord your helper.
Look within and you will find depression
Look back and you will find disappointment
Look around and you will find discouragement
Look up with the eye of faith and deliverance will come
Fetters that bind will be broken
Iron bands that ensnare will be snapped
I have come to set you free.

For each impossible situation you face, My grace is more than sufficient. For every need you have, there is an abundant supply. For every wound, I am the remedy; I am Jehovah Rapha...The Lord who heals. I am Jehovah Nissi...The Lord your Banner, and My banner over you is love.
Come to Me with childlike faith
Come with unselfish desire
Come with a humble and contrite heart
This is the way to overcome.

I will receive and bless you and you too will be

filled with laughter and your lips with **shouts of joy**.

When Israel shouted the shout of faith, Jericho's walls came down and victory was secured.

Shout beloved…Shout! Shout! Shout!

Job 8:21 *Job 13:15* *Psalm 51:17*

PERSONAL VICTORY

_____
_____
_____

A NEW ANOINTING

I anoint your head with oil

My covenant people, this is to be your experience.
A new anointing will invade the sanctuary.

Revival blessing and fire are about to sweep through every area of worship and activity. This anointing will come upon the music, leadership and the church. It will captivate and turn the hearts of many to saving faith in Me.

Just as fervent singing and Spirit-anointed leadership have characterized other awakenings, so also shall this be. My word will continue to be proclaimed with renewed freshness, clarity and power. Old and young will hasten to this house; here, needs will be met in Me. Manna also will be found outside the door of every man's tent, within reach of all.

As you...
   Invest wholeheartedly in the things of the kingdom
   Incorporate and motivate each member of My body
           in the work of the kingdom
      Implement the gifts of the Spirit,
You will invoke My blessing.

Believe Me, My children, I have promised, and I stand by My word to see it fulfilled. My feet are on the mountains...I am ready to descend with blessings abundant for My Blood-washed people.

I send My word to you again...
Whatever things you ask when you pray, believe
that you receive them...**and you shall have them.**

Here your joy is made complete.

Psalm 23:52   Corinthians 9:8   Mark 11:24

PERSONAL PREPARATION

_____
_____
_____

GOD'S SUPREMACY

Many of My people are living under grey skies and gloomy forecasts and see nothing but darkness ahead. I am your Father; yet you sense I am unconcerned and standing afar off...there seems to be no light at the end of the tunnel.

Over the years, My children have experienced the same, but be of good cheer...**All things work together for good to those who love Me.**

Jonah was taken to the deepest depths. He finally came through with praise and adoration on his lips.

Daniel was cast into a den of hungry lions. He was delivered and many who despised Me, rose up and followed Me.

Joseph was thrown into a miry pit in Canaan, was liberated and eventually became prime minister of Egypt.

The devil meant all this for evil, but I turned it around for good.

Beloved! These are only a few whose formidable situations could have driven them to doubt and despair, but they realized **I was there all the time**...
>Running when they were running
>Hurting when they were hurting
>Bleeding when they were bleeding

I wanted them to know that no attack from the enemy could destroy or thwart My purpose for their lives.

My people, if you lean on Me from this day forward and learn to trust Me, I will...

Bring you through victoriously
Lead you in paths you have not known
Make darkness light before you

With renewed strength and vigor you will shout My name from the mountain tops. You will not go back the way you came and you will never be the same again.

Be confident...
No day is dark when you live in the light of My presence
I am the Chief Shepherd. Your conquering, coming King

Psalm 42:5　　　*Psalm 42:11*　　　*Psalm 43:5*

PERSONAL PERSUASION

_____
_____
_____

SPIRITUAL CIRCUMCISION

Within My church much deliberation is given to…
Coalition
Communication
Consolidation
But, if there is to be an inundation of old-time Pentecostal revival, the emphasis must be placed on purging, cleansing and circumcision.
    Circumcision of the heart and soul

Daily, attacks come from various angles…
    The world with all its adverse, dazzling attractions
    The flesh with all its enticing and fascinating facades
    The devil with all his devious delusions

To come against and overcome these…There must be separation…A cutting away…Parting with… This is no simple matter. There will be suffering, but if you are desirous of walking the highway of holiness and living under the anointing of My Holy Spirit, there is no detour. **This is the price.**

Obedience to the Scriptures is the only route. I annunciate, "**My word is as a two edged sword.**" It has a two-fold purpose…
    Cutting away the unnecessary and offending part
    Constraining the enemy while the procedure is in progress

It is here that the inside is revealed.
It is here that the intents of the heart are disclosed

It is here that unresolved issues and tissues are removed. Isaiah speaks of these as wounds, bruises and putrefying sores. To live in healing and victory…It is obligatory to put off the 'old man.' Lay aside every weight and carnal entrapment and be eager to run the race and win.

> If your eye offends you pluck it out
> If your hand offends you cut it off
> If a besetting sin ensnares you…die to it

All of these illustrate the nature and purpose of spiritual circumcision.

I exhort you child of Heaven, place yourself on the altar. Sharpen the edge of the blood- stained stone and allow surgery to begin now. Be assured of pain but be much more assured of great gain.

Ephesians 4:17-24   Matt. 5:27-30   Jeremiah 4:4

SPIRITUAL SURGERY

_____
_____
_____

OUR FATHER

My people

Bless My name for ever and ever, for all power belongs to Me.
> **I change the times and the seasons**
> **I raise up kings and remove kings**
> **I make the sun to shine, the wind to blow,**
> **The grass to grow, and the tides that wash your beaches twice every day**

Beloved, I am your God; wisdom, knowledge and understanding are Mine. **I am your Father,** you are My children and the sheep of My pasture.

I have…
> Invited you to My banqueting table
> Included you in My eternal inheritance
> Integrated you with the angels and archangels of Heaven

I am the God of Abraham, Isaac and Jacob and I have chosen to dwell in you, walk with you and make Myself known through you.

I long to hear from you in
> **Worship and Prayer**

I have created you for My pleasure and delight.
> **Come to Me often**
> **Call upon My name**
> **Cease not to exalt Me above all others**

Lift up your heads and be lifted up you everlasting doors! And **I will come in**, bringing My blessing, which makes rich and adds no sorrow with it.

                  Caring for you always
                  Your Heavenly Father

Daniel 2:20-22   Psalm 79:13   Hebrews 9:15

PERSONAL RELATIONSHIP

_____
_____
_____

RELEASED

I see many who hurt owing to traumatic events of desertion. The pain of separation has reached the point of devastation. Loneliness has become a constant state. Allow Me to take the pain, struggle and bitterness and I will rebuild your confidence and self-respect.

If resentment and retaliation are harbored and nursed in your spirit, they will produce depression and despondency and will rob you of the joy and freedom which are yours in Me.

From this day…
    Release everything that would seek to crush and destroy you.
You will be empowered to forgive…creating within your spirit a longing to move on.

You will be free to…

Live
Trust
Love again

Satan stripped My servant Job of his health, wealth and his wife's affection. I restored his losses and imparted to him twice as much as he previously possessed. **Through it all, he trusted Me** and had this testimony… I blessed his latter days more than his beginning.
My children, I purpose to heal your fractured heart…

Streams Of Sonlight

**Beauty for ashes awaits you
I am the Lord who heals**

Believe...All things are possible

Romans 5:20-21   Isaiah 43:19   Job 13:15

PERSONAL SURRENDER

_____
_____
_____

WEAPONS OF WARFARE

My called out ones

Arm yourselves, as My servant Paul exhorted you to do in the book of Ephesians.

Take up your weapons and put on the whole armor of God, that you may be able to withstand all the wiles of the devil. You wrestle not with flesh and blood but with rulers of darkness and spiritual forces of wickedness. Be perceptive My children, you cannot put on until you first put off.
Put off the old man...the old garment...the old nature and every form of worldly pursuit.

Put on your weapons of warfare; these are not carnal, **but mighty in Me**, to the pulling down of satan's strongholds and every high thing that exalts itself above Me. These, if used wisely and correctly will enable you to...

Overrun
Overcome
Overthrow

Resulting in you becoming victorious in every hostile situation.

I charge you therefore, put on...
The shield of faith...for the protection of vital organs; resisting all the fiery darts of the evil one.

The helmet of salvation...for the defence of your thought area; your dreams and aspirations.

The sword of the Spirit...the offense weapon... My eternal word; wield it in the face of the enemy and he will hastily retreat. Satan is the god of this present world, and the prince of the power of the air. Never underestimate him, he is not a weakling; but, by the **Blood of the cross and the mention of My name**, you can...

     Stop his mouth
     Stay his hand
    Swiftly defeat him

I have given you authority over all the power of the enemy and nothing shall by any means harm you.

Eph. 6:10-20 II Corinthians 10:4 Isaiah 54:17

PERSONAL PREPARATION

_____
_____
_____

REJOICE

Hear Me, My people, you who are washed and sanctified. You who were once alienated but are now part of My kingdom...
I say to you, **Rejoice!**
      Rejoice...My mercy has reached you
   Rejoice...your name is written in the Lamb's Book of Life
     Rejoice...there is a place prepared for you in Heaven
Rejoice...in Me: the great God of Heaven and earth

If you continue to love mercy and do justly, I will guide you in all your ways. When you turn to the left or to the right, you will hear My voice prompting, "This is the way, walk in it."

If you continue to present yourselves as living sacrifices, holy, acceptable to Me, which is your reasonable service, I will rebuke the devourer for your sake and he will depart from you. Then you will prove what is My good, acceptable and perfect will.

If you continue to humble yourselves, I will uplift you. It is a good thing to be clothed with humility, as with a garment. My word attests...I resist the proud, but give grace to the humble.

If you return to Me and determine to walk in the light of My word you will continually and joyfully be blessed. I purpose to renew, refresh and revive you. From this day streams will break forth in your wilderness and wasteland. You shall arise and come to Zion with singing, and everiasting joy shall be on your heads.

Rejoice! Rejoice! I am your,...
Well, when you are thirsty
Bread, when you are hungry
Great Physician, when you are sick
Light, when you walk in darkness
Strength, when you are weak
Deliverer, when you are held in bondage
Comforter, when you are sad and lonely
Anchor, in the time of storm

Luke 10:20   1 Thessalonians 5:16   Psalm 33:1-2

PERSONAL REJOICING

_____
_____
_____

THE NAME OF JESUS

My children

Allow Me to refresh your memory concerning the power and potential of My Son's name. I have highly exalted Him and given Him the name that is above every name.
At His name every knee shall bow and every tongue confess that He is Christ the Lord.

My word teaches you to…
> **Praise the name of Jesus**
> **Pray in the name of Jesus**
> **Preach in the name of Jesus**
> **Perform miracles in the name of Jesus**

Whatsoever you do, do in the name of Jesus. All the authority of Heaven is vested in His name. When you speak His name…

> All Heaven comes to attention
> All hell is subdued
> All that He was…All that He is and all He accomplished defines His pre-eminence.

If you ask anything in His name, He will do it, that I may be glorified in Him.

The name of Jesus affords salvation…for there is no other name under Heaven, given among men, whereby you must be saved.

The name of Jesus enacts healing…In His name

pray, anoint with oil, lay hands on the sick and they shall recover.

The name of Jesus performs the miraculous... Believe in the power of His name and you shall do even greater than you have seen Him do.

The most rewarding and exciting moment of all time will be on that day when you stand before Him at the Bema Judgement. You will wear His name indelibly inscribed on your forehead. Every good shepherd marks his own sheep. You, on that great and notable day will be marked for all eternity.

Colossians 3:17   John 15:16   Revelation 22:4

PERSONAL APPLICATION

_____
_____
_____

SONG OF ENCOURAGEMENT

Sing O heavens!
Break forth into singing, O you mountains. Shout you lower parts of the earth and all you who have breath. I have blotted out as a thick cloud your transgressions. Your sins and iniquities I remember no more.

Be glad! I have...
> **Engulfed you in My love**
> **Enrolled you in My book of remembrance**
> **Endowed you with My Holy Spirit**

Do not permit the enemy to divert or defeat you. When the pressures of the world and attacks of the evil one threaten to destroy you, **My strength will be your all-sufficiency**.
When Moses came to the Red Sea with three and a half million people, there was no way forward and no way to retreat...
> **Where there was no way, I made a way**

I pushed back the waters of that mighty Red Sea and My people walked over on dry ground.

When the Israelites encamped in the wilderness and no food was available, a miracle was executed and manna was provided for forty years.

Beloved, I not only make a way, but **I am the way** and I make provision for all those who love Me.

Enter into My presence with thanksgiving.

Worship and bow down before Me...Sing to Me a new song...Proclaim My salvation among the people and I, the Lord, will be your strength and stay.

Isaiah 44:22-23   *Psalm 32:11*   *James 4:7*

PERSONAL PROVISION

_____
_____
_____

THE DELUGE PROMISE

Covenant people

I call upon you to remember the former things no more, neither consider the things of old. Behold! I will do a new thing. It shall spring forth speedily and you will see it together. I will send rivers from which My people shall drink and be bountifully satisfied. They shall come from My throne to the church, with blessing, healing, anointing and fruitfulness, wherever the waters flow.

Put aside your preconceived ideas and traditional formalities, for this shall be
A new thing

Prepare for a new direction and a new dynamic, expansion time has come. Riverbanks are about to burst, bringing **the deluge** that will impact every corner of the earth. I will make haste to see it accomplished. Believe Me, My people, I am not a man that I should lie. I have spoken and I will make it good. I have promised blessing and it will not be reversed. There will be on every high mountain and in every low valley, rivers and streams of water in the day of My visitation.

I require...
Renewed faith in My promises
Complete obedience to My voice
Total commitment to My cause
and hearts full of praise and gratitude toward Me.

The realization of these will result in immense joy and delight to My heart.

Look up! Look around!
There is...
Rumbling in the heavens
Rustling in the mulberry trees
Receptiveness in My church
The sky is now dark with clouds...
Run! Put out your water pots, there is the sound of **abundance of rain**.

Isaiah 43:19   1 Kings 18:44   Ezekiel 47:1-12

PERSONAL COMMITMENT

_____
_____
_____

ARISE MY LOVE

Arise My love

Society today cries out for love. My people cry out for love. I also, cry out for love...For more and more love from those who...
>**Turn away from sin**
>**Own My name**

There are different concepts of love in the world, all of which can be expressed and enjoyed in various measures. Most are short-lived because they are carnal, self-gratifying, and have no undergirding or permanent stability. None of these bear any resemblance of the original. **My love for you is not of that category...**
>**It is Agape...It is Divine...it excels all others**

It is unselfish, sacrificial and unchanging. Only a true believer can grasp its significance.
>Its origin has its seat in the courts of Heaven
>Its object is the soul of sinful man
>Its magnitude far exceeds what tongue can tell

It was manifested in Bethlehem's manger where I laid aside My kingly robes and was made in the likeness of sinful flesh.

It was demonstrated on Calvary's mountain where I took your place, paid your debt and died that you might have life and have it more abundantly.

It was displayed at Bethany when I was caught up into the clouds. As I left My bewildered and

frightened disciples I gave them My pledge...
Fear not little flock, I am not leaving you abandoned. I will come again and receive you to Myself.

It was declared by My servant, Paul, when he said, "While you were still sinners, Christ died for you."

There was nothing in you, My love, that commended you. You walked in darkness and without hope; nevertheless, My all-sufficient love went out after you and...
Saved you
Sanctified you
Set you in a place near to the heart of My Father

Cherished one, My love for you has not abated, I love you dearly and I jealously long to have you for Myself.
You are the apple of My eye
My chosen...My joy...My chief delight
You are My bride...My fair one
You are beautiful! Arise! Come away with Me, for intimacy is on My agenda.

There is nothing in Heaven, on earth, or under the earth that can separate you from this eternal, incomparable, agape love.

Come therefore My beloved, lean on Me and share the secrets of your inmost being. In return, I will divulge the plans I have for you.
I sought you...

**bought you...
brought you into My banqueting house and
My banner over you is love**

Song of Solomon 2:10   Jer. 31:3   1 John 4:10

PERSONAL DEVOTION

_____
_____
_____

THE ENTRANCE

OF YOUR WORDS

GIVES LIGHT

Psalm 119:130

TO BE SURE

As My eyes go to and fro throughout the earth I note you doubting your salvation and the benefits which are yours to claim. Therefore, I urge you... Delve into the Scriptures, for in them you can know you have eternal life.

I have called you by your name, you are Mine I have washed and sanctified you through My Blood

Delve into the book of Psalms...Here I assure you I have put a new song in your mouth, even praise to Me.

Delve into the books of My prophets...Here it is revealed, I have given you a new heart and new spirit, giving strength to prevail.

Delve into the Mosaic books...In these is promised a Redeemer, One who will come and set men free.

Delve into the book of Job...Perceive a new hope for the future and say with him, "I know that my Redeemer lives...In my flesh I shall see God."

Delve into the New Testament, My New Covenant...Here you are offered an open line of communication with Me.

Delve into the book of Acts and the letters of the apostles...Here I confirm, you are a new creation through the operation of the Holy Spirit.

Delve into the book of Revelation, here it records, the believer is given...
**A new name
A new environment...In the New Jerusalem**

And it will come to pass that there will be one house...My House, where there is no sickness, sorrow or sighing . I dwell there and will wipe away all tears from your eyes.

Be sure My people, be sure, it is well with your soul

1 John 5:13   Revelation 21:4   2 Corinthians 5:17

PERSONAL RESPONSE

_____
_____
_____

FAITH TRIUMPHS

My children

It has come up before Me that your faith is failing…doubts and fears are creeping in. Fear not, My promise still stands firm and good…
> **Lo I am with you always, even to the end**

Do not be misguided; **faith is required**. Faith is the sum total of your survival.

By faith, My people Israel were delivered from the cruel hand of Egypt's Pharaoh.

By faith, David was spared the sharp edge of Goliath's sword.

By faith, the three Hebrew children were rescued from the burning flames of the fiery furnace.

These were My physically circumcised people… Shall I do less for My spiritually circumcised? No! No!
> **You are My prized possession**
> **My peculiar people**

For you I poured out all My love and I will give you power over all the power of the enemy. Satan will capitulate when he hears your voice and sees you coming; he will recognize that you **come in My name**. He comprehends that in My name every demon must flee. He is mindful that My name is

above all other names, in Heaven and on earth.
I am your...

Shield and buckler
Fortress and strong tower
Refuge and strength

No weapon forged on the anvils of hell can touch or harm you. At all times I am watching over you, your best interests are close to My heart.

Starve your doubts and they will vanish like the morning dew
Feed your faith and your soul will prosper

Hebrews 11:6   Colossians 2:10-11   Psalm 91:4

PERSONAL TRIUMPH

_____
_____
_____

PRAISE AND WORSHIP

Hear O Israel, My chosen
I am the Alpha and Omega

With My hand I laid the foundations of the earth.
With My right hand I stretched out the heavens.
With the word of My mouth every living creature was brought into being.
Before the world was, you were continually on My mind. You were part of My eternal program.

I, the Lord created you

Before you were born, I formed you in the womb. I made you in My likeness and your chief end is to honor and glorify Me.

In your generation I desire to live, reign and establish My kingdom among all peoples, nations and tongues.
Therefore...
Proclaim My name
Lift up My name
Glorify My name

I exhort you...
    Leap as the deer on the mountains
    Shine as the stars in the firmament
    Sing as the birds of the air
Shout aloud and celebrate My name. Praise and worship Me with the trumpet, the flute, stringed instruments and loud cymbals. Let everything that

has breath praise Me; I dwell in the center of the praises of My people. You are My friends and My beloved.

Sing praise to your King, sing praise

Isaiah 51:13   Psalm 150:1-6   1Cor. 6:11

PERSONAL PRAISE

_____
_____
_____

MY KINGDOM

Seek first My kingdom. Seek and enter by the...

Eye of faith...Lift up your eyes and behold the One who left the glory, laid down His life and lives today to make intercession for you.

Step of faith...Move out on My promise, believing if you come to Me as you are, I will not turn you away.

Hand of faith...Place your hand in Mine knowing that I, who put the sun, moon and stars in their places have pledged that no man shall pluck you out of My hand.

You enter the kingdom, understanding, that no man having put his hand to the plough and turns back is fit for the kingdom, neither is everyone who cries daily, "Lord, Lord." It is he who endures to the end that shall be saved.

To you who have entered, I implore you to take a renewed and dedicated interest in the work of the kingdom.
**Grow and increase in the kingdom
Influence unbelievers for the kingdom
Intercede on behalf of those within the kingdom**

Invade the enemy's territory by putting on the whole armor and fighting the battle to the gate. I have entrusted you with the good tidings of the

kingdom and I insist on unity within the ranks. It is written, every kingdom divided against itself is brought to desolation and every house divided against itself will not stand.
In observing these principles, blessing will be overwhelmingly poured out. This was My covenant with Abraham, it is also My covenant with you.

It is for all who...
>Believe the promises
>Fulfill the conditions
>Reach out in faith

and become witnesses and examples to all peoples.

I have delegated authority to every believer to go and preach the kingdom, heal the sick and cast out demons.

My word affirms that this gospel of the kingdom must be preached to every tribe, tongue and nation...The earth will then be filled with the knowledge of My glory, as the waters cover the sea and I shall be known as...

King of kings and Lord of lords

Matthew 6:33   Psalm 133:1   Isaiah 11:6-10

PERSONAL CONCLUSION

_____
_____
_____

RIVERS OF RENEWAL

Behold! I see rivers of water flowing.

In these there is life. My children, when you see the waters, do not be fearful or fainthearted, they are released to you by the Holy Spirit who wants to make them real in your life. The purpose of the rivers is to bring renewal and revival to My church. They will convey healing and reconciliation to weary and hurting hearts.

All over the world...
> **A Wind is blowing**
> **A Fire is glowing**
> **A River is flowing**

This is that which was spoken by My prophet Ezekiel...
"A river shall come out of the temple, under the threshold and flow down into the valley."
This manifestation is displaying an awesome awareness of My sovereign power and presence. It is divinely and richly supplied. It is moving freely throughout the land, abounding in blessing and generating a new hunger and thirst in the lives of My people.

Believe Me! You are standing on the brink of a new and mighty move of My Spirit. This will be in answer to volumes of ascended prayer and will impact every spectrum of society. Prayer is not only **a key**... it is **the only key**.

Economic and communal decay have been prevalent, but this is changing, socially, politically and spiritually. People of all persuasions will eagerly attend the place of worship and call on My name. This is the purpose and potency of the gospel enacted.

Let go of apprehension and restriction, and the river with all its streams will begin flowing toward you. The Spirit and the bride say, "Let him who is thirsty come and take of the Water of Life freely, and he who drinks, out of him shall flow rivers of living water."

When the river surges…Ankle deep…knee deep… waist deep…The time has come to launch out into the river and swim.

Ezekiel 47:1-5   Luke 5:4   Revelation 22:17

PERSONAL RENEWAL

_____
_____
_____

THE LORD REIGNS

I am the Lord who reigns in power...

With My wisdom I founded the earth
With My understanding I established the heavens
With My knowledge the depths were broken up and the clouds dropped their dew. This unveiling is to promote renewal and refreshing in the hearts of those who are walking the rough and winding road of fear and failure. Let it be known that failure in the past does not impede you today.

My word has stated...
Even the youths may faint and young men utterly fail but they that wait on the Lord shall renew their strength, they shall mount up with wings like eagles, they shall run and not be weary, they shall walk and not faint.

Be assured, I will...
Unravel the confusion
Unfold the truth
Unlock closed doors and permit you to walk through

My people, when satan devises evil against you; stand firm!
The mighty power that ...
Raised Me from the dead
Put all things under My feet
Seated Me at My Father's right hand
is available to you who have acknowledged Me as

Savior and Lord.

That same power brings…
Order out of chaos
Water out of the rock
Coins from the mouth of the fish
And more significantly…**Sinful men from satan's subtle grip**

Lift up your gates and the King of glory will come in. I am the King and reign in righteousness and power over all the earth, and of My kingdom there shall be no end.

A song of praise ascends from the hearts of My people…
"Alleluia! For the Lord our God the omnipotent reigns."

Isaiah 32:1   Luke 1:32-33   Revelation 19:6

PERSONAL AFFIRMATION

_____
_____
_____

FEAR NOT

Fear not resonates throughout My word, reminding you, that in Me all your fears can be dispelled.
I have not given you the spirit of fear but of love, power and a sound mind

You fear for families, finances and the future...Fear not, I am with you, be not dismayed, **I am** your **God**.
              'I Am' is My name
I am...
    The God of Abraham, the One who provides for those who learn to trust Me

The God of Daniel, the One who protects those who are called to walk through the lions' den

The God of Joseph, the One who preserves and prospers those, who in simple faith, leave the choice with Me

The God of the Bible, the One who is able to perform that which is promised
My word shall not return to Me void.

I am with you, I will advance before you and make the crooked places straight and the rough places smooth. I will shelter you in the secret place of My pavilion and deliver in six troubles; yes, even in seven no evil shall touch you. Be prepared! Serving Me does not insulate you from the harsh realities and untoward occurrences of life, as My servants of the past have proved...

Abraham walked the road of obedience and sacrifice.

Job walked the road of loneliness and ridicule.

Paul walked the road of persecution and false accusation.

These all fought a good fight and finished the course, and each could confidently say, "**The Lord stood by me.**"

Isaiah 41:10   Exodus 3:14   Psalm 91:9-16

PERSONAL CONFIDENCE

_____
_____
_____

PREPARE FOR BATTLE

My ransomed ones

Realize afresh that we are at war with the enemy of souls. We are in conflict with the forces of evil, darkness, principalities and powers. I call on you to rise out of your comfort zone and enlist in active service today. Do not be alarmed by the cunning schemes of your adversary, the devil.

My word is truth

The gates of hell shall not prevail against you. It is recorded; one with Me shall chase a thousand, and two with Me shall chase ten thousand.
**You will overcome. You will win
You fight in the strength of your King**

Your strategy is not simply to defend, but to attack; to root up and pull down the citadels and strongholds of satan.

I will be to you…
**As an army with banners
A mighty warrior
A triumphant monarch**
Before Me, is My sceptre, high and lifted up. I have anointed and appointed you to follow in My footsteps…
In the train of My triumph

Do not be filled with trepidation by him who is

come to steal, kill and destroy.

I have...
> **Encircled you with My love**
> **Enriched you by My grace**
> **Encamped My holy angels around you**

and no encounter with the oppressor shall obscure your awareness of My presence.

My children, be unwavering...
> Raise your banners
> Do battle with the enemy
> Bring home the spoil

I have prevailed...
> **Yours is the victory!**

11 Cor. 10:4   Matthew 16:18   Isaiah 35:10

PERSONAL READINESS

_____
_____
_____

HELP

Beloved

I perceive you are hurting because of those who have abused and mistreated you. Some have been spurned and rejected, others misunderstood and misjudged. No one was ill-treated and spurned more than My Son. Agents of satan attempted to eliminate Him...
>In the cradle
>In the crowd
>On the cross

but none prevailed.
He knew He was girded by love.

Love led Him...
>**To Calvary**
>**To the tomb**
>**To Heaven**

That same love understands your plight, knows the mistreatment and feels the pain. My child, I have seen your tears and heard your cries. Reach out in faith, believing, and I will heal your wounded spirit. Cry out to Me now and I will send My word to heal you.

In John's Gospel, the woman with the issue of blood who pressed through the crowd and stretched out to touch the hem of My Son's garment was made entirely whole. I invite you to push through every obstacle and you too will experience My healing.

He who comes to Me, must believe that I am and that I reward those who diligently seek Me.

I will help you and that right early. To you who fear My name; I am the Sun of Righteousness, risen, with healing in My wings. I am the glory and the lifter of your head.

Isaiah 53:5   Psalm 121:1   Jeremiah 31:3

PERSONAL AFFIRMATION

_____
_____
_____

WHO IS HE?

Who is He that...
>Laid the foundations of the earth?
>Stretches out the heavens like a curtain?
>Counts the stars and calls them all by name?

Who is He that...
>Gathers the wind in His hands?
>Stills the waters and calms the storm?
>Forms the clouds and makes the rain to fall?
>Gives life and significance to all His creation?

Who is He that...
>Picked you up?
>Cleaned you up?
>Tuned you up and is returning soon to take you up?
>**It is I, your Lord and King**
>**I am sovereign and I am holy**

Even the angels cry out in My presence, "**Holy, holy, holy, Lord God Almighty. The whole earth is full of Your glory.**"

My name is...
>**Abba...Father**
>**Creator, Upholder and Sustainer of all things**
>**Your Passover Lamb and Great High Priest**
>**Jehovah Shalom...The Lord your peace**

I am the One who...
>**Blessed the children**
>**Forgave the sinner**
>**Healed the sick**
>**Raised the dead**

I invite you...
Come away with Me and rest a while. Cast aside the anxieties of financial stress, physical sickness, domestic demands and emotional problems. Lay them one by one at My feet and allow Me to bear them away. Come, all who labor and are heavy laden and I will give you rest. My yoke is easy and My burden is light. **There is a guaranteed rest for My covenant people**.

Psalm 102:25   Proverbs 30:4   John 8:11

PERSONAL PERCEPTION

_____
_____
_____

OLD OR NEW

Who is...
>Wonderful in counsel?
>Excellent in wisdom?
>Mighty in Israel?

It is I, the Lord...The King of glory, the Creator of all things great and small.

My little children, this shall be for you a year of celebration
Your eyes will behold Me in all My beauty

Great expressions of My love and mercy shall be exhibited in everything around you. My Spirit will come upon you, as in the days of the early church. You will comprehend a new awareness of My presence, accompanied by a new revelation of divine power.

I will impart a new appetite for...
>**Personal participation**
>**Newness**
>**Wholeness**
>**Counsel and direction**

These attributes will be the hallmark of those who forsake the old paths and walk in the new.

Be resolute; do not look back and cling to the old, launch out into the new. I have vowed, the latter will be greater than the former.
The new song I have given you shall come forth as

never before. You will come and go from this place finding good and pleasant pastures.

Lift up your hearts and welcome that which is new
For this day I created you
For this day you were born

Psalm 24:7-9   Acts 2:17   Matthew 18:19

PERSONAL CHOICE

_____
_____
_____

EVERLASTING

Hear O Israel and all who follow after uprightness. My ransomed ones shall return to Zion. Good tidings have come from the realms of Heaven.

Your Redeemer has come...
    Salvation will visit My people
    Comfort will come in time of trouble
    Waste places will blossom as a fruitful garden
    Rivers will flow in the desert

My name is Wonderful, Counselor, Mighty God, Everlasting Father and Prince of Peace. My going forth is as of old, from everlasting to everlasting. All that I am and have is everlasting.
    My everlasting love is assured for all men.
    My everlasting salvation is procured for all men
    My everlasting kingdom is secured for all men

Lift up your voice in adoration, out of Israel has come a...
        Ruler
        King
        Savior
A Savior...who saves to the uttermost.

I will bring out those who sit in darkness and heal those who are broken-hearted.
The blind will see, the lame walk and all who are held captive I shall gloriously liberate.

Prepare a way for My coming. Make straight in the

desert a highway for your God. Let every valley be exalted and every mountain be made low, the earth will then shine with the light of My glory.

> All flesh will see it
> Creation will rejoice in it
> Heaven will be glad because of it
> **I will be magnified**

John 3:16   *Hebrews 13:20*   *Isaiah 9:6*

PERSONAL ANTICIPATION

_____
_____
_____

COVENANT BLESSING

The time has come to move out into My promised covenant blessing. If you listen attentively to My voice and keep My commandments, turn not to the left or right, walk before Me with clean hands and pure heart...

My presence will go before you to overthrow and scatter those who buffet you. I will never forsake you.
My peace will be your portion. It is written...I will keep you in perfect peace as your mind is stayed on Me.
My provision will be more than you require. I provide daily for the...
>Birds of the air
>Beast of the field
>Fish of the sea

I shall supply much more for you, My people.

My servant David records, "**The Lord is My Shepherd, I shall not want**... I have been young and now I am old, yet I have not seen the righteous forsaken or his children begging bread."
>My eyes are upon you
>My ears are open to your cry
>My compassions fail not; they are new every morning

>No oppressor shall offend you
>No plague shall come near your home

Your enemies shall come against you one way, and

flee before you seven ways, bearing witness that you own My name.

I have purchased for you a new and better covenant...
    Redemption for all who repent of sin and believe the Gospel
    Resurrection from the dead for all born-again believers
    Rewards for those who witness a good confession and continue to the end
    Reunion with those who died in 'the faith' and have been promoted to Glory
    Reigning with Me in My everlasting kingdom for ever

Deut. 28:1-14   *Psalm 24:4*   *Hebrews 12:24*

PERSONAL PROVISION

_____
_____
_____

THEN CAME THE MORNING

Children of Zion

As you come into My presence, I reveal to you afresh that **I am the Lamb of God** who takes away the sin of the world. I am the One who walked the winepress of My Father's wrath and judgement alone.

Upon My head are many crowns
Over My scarred body is a robe dipped in precious Blood
Across My brow and over My thigh a name is written, King of kings and Lord of lords

I am the One who...
    Walked the Via Dolorosa
    Climbed the hill of Golgotha
I am the One who was lifted up on Calvary's cross and cried out with final breath, "Father, it is finished, into Your hands I commend My Spirit."

Later that day My body was removed from the cross, wrapped in fine linen and laid in a borrowed tomb.
Pilate ordered...
    "Seal the stone
    Secure the tomb
    Set the guard"
Then came the morning...Early on the third day, I arose from the tomb, victorious over hell, death and the grave. I was seen in the garden, in Galilee and

the disciples.
worshiped Me, and called
God."
as that same Jesus.

own way of suffering
our own cross
not alone. I, your
Lord Jesus, will console

Me, so it will come for
for some disappointed,
frustrated disciples, the sun came up and seeing me standing on the shore they cried out, "It is the Lord!"

Weeping may endure for a night but joy comes in the morning

Revelation 17:14   John 21:4-7   Matthew 28:5-6

PERSONAL EXPECTATION

_____
_____
_____

REVIVAL BLESSING

Church of the firstborn

You are living in a time when people have no thought of Me or eternal things. They are buying, selling and laying up treasure as though they will live forever.
                   My house is unattended
                  My book is seldom opened
 My name is not mentioned, unless it is blasphemed. The world is hastening on toward the same state as Sodom and Gomorrah. Judgement was poured out and not one soul escaped, save for Lot and his family.

The crying need of the world today is...
           The sound of abundance of rain
Elijah in his day required natural showers...
           Your requirement is spiritual showers

 A downpour today is fundamental for a revival that will save souls, clean up society and refresh the hearts of My Blood-washed people. Be motivated, I am more ready to give than you are to receive. If I spared not My Son but delivered Him up for mankind, shall I not with Him also freely give you all things?

There are conditions to be fulfilled by those who are called by My name...
        Repent, and your sins will be blotted out
        Bring all the tithes into the storehouse

Humble yourselves and seek My face in prayer

When these conditions are observed, I will show you the great and exceeding riches of My grace and power. **You will hear the sound…see the great sight**…Clouds bursting around you, falling in blessing on your head. You will cry out with Moses, "Stand still and see the salvation of the Lord." Redeemed ones, this is the passionate desire of My heart.

Let faith rise up within you

Habakkuk 3:2   Psalm 85:6   1 Kings 18:41

PERSONAL DEDICATION

_____
_____
_____

MAN OF SORROWS

Is it nothing to you, all you who pass by?

Take heed and see if there is any sorrow like unto My sorrow. Sorrow which My Father laid on Me on the day of His fierce anger and fury. All My enemies have heard of My affliction. They have scoffed, clapped their hands, hissed, shaken their heads and pulled the hairs from My face. I am a Man of sorrows and acquainted with grief. Surely, I have borne your grief and carried your sorrows.

Their wickedness and sin have been laid on Me. I have been oppressed, afflicted and cut off from the land of the living. I was led as a lamb to the slaughter and as a sheep before its shearer is silent, I did not open My mouth. For the transgression of My people I have been slain.

It pleased the Lord to bruise Me
It is He who has placed Me on the altar
It is He who has made My soul an offering for sin
I shall see...
The fruit of My labors
The enemy take flight as many sons are brought to glory
By My knowledge many shall be justified

Take heart, My people, **your King is not in the grave** as others are. I have been raised from the dead and have risen on high. I hold in My hands the keys of hell, death and the grave. The opposition is defeated and Heaven's door is open wide.

Be immovable in your faith, lean wholly on Me, knowing that I have loved, redeemed and sealed you with My Holy Spirit of promise.
**I have taken your place
Paid your debt
My vicarious death proclaims that you may go out free**
By My stripes you are healed.

Lamentations 1:12   Isaiah 53:6   Revelation 1:5-6

PERSONAL GRATITUDE

_____
_____
_____

MY PRESENCE

My heart goes out to you...

Your name and needs are known to Me. Do not be apprehensive, I will be your sword and shield, will hold your hand and guide you with My eye.
**My love is never ending
My grace, flowing out to you is all sufficient
My mercies come down like dewdrops, new every morning**

Let not the winds of adversity hinder your devotion to Me.
Let not the world entice you into its ways.
Let not the wiles of satan deter you in your pursuit of righteousness.
My presence within you will conquer that which may come against you.

When a daughter of Israel was found in adultery and about to be stoned to death...
My presence brought deliverance.

When the widow of Nain walked in the funeral procession of her only son...
My presence gave life.

When the supply of wine came to an end at the wedding of Cana in Galilee...
My presence miraculously provided.

When you were still in sin...

My presence brought salvation and joy.

In My presence there is fullness of joy and at My right hand there are pleasures for evermore.
When you pass through deep waters they shall not overflow you. When you walk through the fire, you will not be burned. I, the Holy One of Israel will be there to deliver.

When you pass through the valley of the shadow of death, I will be with you. My rod and staff will comfort and uphold you until you are absent from the body, and in My immediate presence.

I am Jehovah Shamah...In your midst

Lamentations 3:23   Exodus 33:14   Matthew 28:18

PERSONAL CONFIDENCE

_____
_____
_____

BEHOLD!

Behold! Behold! A new thing will be done for you and you shall know that its source is in Me.

Members of the household of faith...
As sure as sparks fly upwards from the anvil and as sure as the rain falls from the heavens, so sure am I ready to bless you. I desire to pour out upon you the latter rain foretold by My servants, and though it tarry, wait for it, for it shall surely come. A mighty onrush of blessing will be released from heaven and you will not be able to contain it.

There will be a...
        Repentance unknown in the church
        Restoration unequalled in the church
        Revival unparalleled in the church
This will touch down in your midst and move throughout the land; even the uttermost parts will feel the vibrations. My name will be uplifted and greatly magnified.

        Sinners will be converted
        Shackles broken
        The deaf shall hear
        The blind see
Broken hearts and bodies will be made completely whole
The dead will be raised and life-threatening diseases terminated, demons cast out and the tormented and oppressed will go out free
Free to love, follow and **serve Me**

When these things come to pass and My word has covered the earth, I will see of the travail of My soul and be satisfied. Then shall My return be at hand.

Now, it behooves My people to...
> Bind the strong man and spoil his goods
> Buy the field and secure the treasure
> Bring in the nets and savor the catch

Know that no effort made in My name, goes unnoticed, unblessed or without reward.

Behold! I have pledged My word and stand by it to see it realized

Hebrews 2:3   Matthew 12:28-29   Hosea 6:3

PERSONAL CONTEMPLATION

_____
_____
_____

DIVINE ATTACHMENT

My children

You were created for My pleasure and eternal glory...
**I planned and prepared for you
I called you by your name and set My seal upon you**
I am your portion and long for you to be blessed, healed and notably set free.
**Free in body
Free in spirit
Free from every entity that binds and hinders you from ascending into heavenly places**

My design is that you flourish, prosper and be fruitful in every good work, identifying My will, and exercising My power in your life. This is conditional on your **divine attachment** to Me. If you abide in Me and My words abide in you, you may ask what you will and it shall be done for you. Abiding in Me culminates in bearing much fruit, for without Me you can do nothing. The devil is aware of this unfailing affinity with Me, and is consistently manoeuvring schemes whereby he can render this relationship void.
Do not...
**Fear
Lose hope
Let go of confidence, which has great reward**

Do not grieve the Holy Spirit by whom you were

anointed. I have prayed for you that you may be kept and that nothing will dissuade you from implementing My plan.

You are strengthened with all might according to My glorious power; that same power that raised Me from the dead and seated Me at My Father's right hand and gave Me a name above every other name, that at My name every knee should bow and every tongue confess that
I am Christ the Lord

Ephesians 1:4-6   Colossians 1:10   John 15:7

PERSONAL GRATITUDE

_____
_____
_____

IN THE MIDST

Children of Zion

I delight to be in your midst…
As a boy **I stood in the midst** of the teachers in the temple. I desired to be with those who had an ardent interest in the work of the kingdom.

When I died on the cross, **I was placed in the midst** of two thieves…
There I revealed My love and transforming grace, this being the supreme objective of My mission to the world.

When I arose from the dead, **I stood in the midst** of My disciples…
I yearned to impart to them My peace which passes all understanding and the reality that in Me there is eternal life. Because I live you shall live also. **I am He that lives and was dead and I am alive for evermore**.

Today in Heaven, **I stand in the midst** of the seven candlesticks…
Shining in the strength and brightness of My Father's glory.

I want the nations to know, **I am that Light which shall never be extinguished**. I am the Light that lights every man who comes into the world and he that follows Me shall not walk in darkness.

In your midst is where I continually long to be...
That is where My heart is
Where My life's Blood was shed
Where I shall soon set up My kingdom and reign with you forever
Until then, keep yourselves unspotted from the world. Put off the works of darkness and put on love, kindness and peace.

I stand in your midst today as Savior, Lord and coming King.

Be motivated to...
Eagerly and earnestly intensify your devotion to Me
Walk daily and consistently with Me
Unceasingly lift up My name in the church where My people gather together to worship Me
My promise remains; where two or three are gathered together in My name, there I am in the midst.

Meet Me there!

Shalom

Psalm 46:5   Revelation 7:14   Matthew 28:10

PERSONAL COMMITMENT

_____
_____
_____

I WILL RETURN

Beloved, in the book of Daniel, I have proclaimed that a day is fast approaching when those who have been wise and obeyed My precepts will glow as the brightness of Heaven. Those who have turned many to righteousness shall shine as the stars forever.

The godly in the grave will awaken to receive their allotted inheritance and you who are alive will join with them as they rise to meet Me in the air. Together I will transport you to My Father's house, and forever you shall be with Me.

My word ratifies that this day is to be remembered as a day of...
> **Reaping...the reapers will take away the wheat and leave the tares**
> **Rewarding...when every believer receives a crown of righteousness**
> **Reckoning...judgement and wrath will be meted out on unbelievers**

To the redeemed at My right hand, My words shall be, "Enter into the joy prepared for you before the foundation of the world."

To the unbelievers at My left hand, I will say, "Depart from Me, I never knew you."

Do not be beguiled or disillusioned...
> **My return is imminent**

It is to be...

Sure...I have said I will return and take you to the place prepared for you.
Swift...Every saint will be caught up and changed in the twinkling of an eye.
Solemn...Two shall be together grinding at the mill, one shall be taken and the other left behind.
Silent...I am coming as a thief in the night to take My bride away.
My children, this day shall be the culmination of all that you have believed and lived for. Ensuing this, for all who have shunned My name and spurned My love, there will be untold gloom and darkness. Fire will go before Me and burn up all My enemies.

Unimaginable lightening will appear in the sky. Mountains and hills will melt like wax at My judicial presence. The heavens shall shout aloud, proclaiming My virtuousness and indescribable power. Every unbeliever on the earth will witness the magnitude of My glory and extent of My fury and wrath. Multitudes...I say multitudes, will call on the rocks and mountains to cover and hide them from My face, as I sit upon My Great White Throne.

Repent and believe

Daniel 12:1-3   John 14:3   Revelation 9:7-10

PERSONAL POSITION

_____
_____
_____

GIFTS ANYONE?

In times past I have spoken to My people through prophets, priests, seers and sages. Today I speak to you who believe through the operation of the Holy Spirit in…

Signs and wonders
Dreams and visions
Spiritual gifts distributed to the body

These are given as the Spirit wills.

I admonish you; do not neglect the gift that is placed within you. This is issued to each of you and can only be improved with regular use.

I counsel you, **stir up the gift** I have committed to you. 'Stirring up' is symbolic of reviving a fire by removing the cinders and blowing into the smouldering embers, thus rekindling the fire. In the same manner, I ask that you allow Me to work in your life and blow by My Spirit upon your gift, that you may not quench Him as He seeks to live and reign within you.

It is My will that you assiduously grow in your gifting, character and in Christian maturity. This will be marked by brokenness, selflessness and a compassion which originates only by the indwelling and infilling of the Holy Spirit. I urge that you desire spiritual gifts and covet earnestly the best. This is not an option; it is My command to every born-again, Spirit-filled believer.

Many who are called by My name are at ease in

Zion, while My people are in dire need of comfort, encouragement, direction and exhortation. There is...
>Famine within their hearts
>Dearth within their souls

They wander from east to west, and run to and fro throughout the land, seeking a word from Me but fail to find it. My children perish for lack of knowledge and understanding.

My gifted ones, may your quest be to excel in the nurturing of the church. Rise! Stir up your gift, make it available for My Spirit to bless and employ. In this way...
>**My people will be edified**
>**My church multiplied**
>**My name glorified**

1 Corinthians 12:11   1 Timothy 4:14   1 Cor. 13:2

PERSONAL GIFTING

_____
_____
_____

THE THINGS I HAVE DONE

Recall, and rejoice in the things I have done.

I formed you…You did not come into being by chance…You are not mass- produced…You did not evolve from animals, or emerge from the sea.
I wanted you
I waited for you
I waged war against the enemy that I might win you
Now you are mine and My stamp of ownership is upon your life

I found you when you were in the world…
Lost in sin
Gripped and entangled in self-indulgence
Walking in darkness, knowing not the truth
My love went out to you, wooing and winning your heart

I forgave you and took your sins which were many…
Buried them in the depths of the deepest sea, where they shall be remembered no more against you
The book of Psalms records…As far as the east is from the west, so far have I removed your transgressions from you

I freed you from the…
Penalty of sin
Power of sin
And one day I will free you from the presence of sin

Streams Of Sonlight

I will escort you all the way from earth to glory, where nothing that defiles shall ever enter in.

I fostered you...With My word I have fed and nurtured you
   By My Spirit I led, anointed and emboldened you
    By My right hand I upheld and supported you
   Night and day the pillars of My presence have succored you

I will fashion you
I know that you...
Love Me
Live for Me
Look for Me
Your citizenship is established in Heaven; from where you await My return. Your mortal body will then be fashioned like unto My glorious body

Psalm 49:5   Luke 15:6   Philippians 3:21

PERSONAL REFLECTION

_____
_____
_____

THE POWER OF THE BLOOD

Never underestimate the value, validity and verdict of My Blood. Without My broken body and shed Blood there is no remission for sin. I pronounced over Israel, "When I see the Blood, I will pass over you."

It is the Blood alone that atones for the soul

My Blood is...
Precious Blood
Poured-out Blood
Powerful Blood
Power, which is still untold, untapped and unending. Nothing on earth, above the earth or under the earth can stand against it. The children of Israel placed the blood of the firstborn lamb on the lintels and doorposts of their homes and the angel of death could do them no harm.

My Blood has many aspects of power, it has...

Redeeming power
You are not redeemed with corruptible things such as silver or gold, but with the precious Blood.

Cleansing power
If you walk in the light as I am in the light, My Blood cleanses you from all sin.

Pacifying power
You have peace through the Blood that was shed on Calvary's cross.

Overcoming power

My people overcame satan, by the power of the Blood and the word of their testimony.

Song-inspiring power

My people sang a new song...
"You are worthy O Lord...For You were slain...You have redeemed us by Your Blood...You have made us kings and priests...We shall reign with You for ever and ever.
Worthy is the Lamb."

1 Peter1:18   1 John 1:7   Revelation 12:11

PERSONAL APPLICATION

_____
_____
_____

REDISCOVER

Church of the redeemed

I am calling you today to…
> **Renew your spiritual vitality**
> **Reopen closed up wells**
> **Rediscover your apostolic origins**

Only in this way can old-time revival blessing be poured out.

Renewing spiritual vitality entails walking the ancient paths, strengthening the feeble knees and making level paths for your feet to tread. This will be attained when you abandon your own ideologies and acquaint yourself with My inspired word. Knowing, loving and being obedient to My word opens the windows of Heaven and brings an overflow of blessing, producing health, wholeness, purity and power.

Reopening closed up wells requires the removal of all mud, mire, silt and slime.
> **The eradication of these is contingent upon My moving in…**

Let this be your removal day.
Say farewell to all trace of self and sin and allow My precious Blood to do its cleansing and creative work. Cry out in the words of My servant David, "Create within Me a clean heart O God…Wash me and I shall be clean…Purge me and I shall be whiter than snow…For I acknowledge my transgression… My sin is ever before me."

Rediscovering your apostolic origins involves...
Humbling yourself before Me
Seeking implicitly after Me
Calling out earnestly to Me

Lord will you not...
Rend the heavens and come down?
Revive us again that your people may rejoice in You?
Open the windows of Heaven and let Your blessing fall?

My children, these are the old paths, nothing less will...
Touch My heart
Open My hand and pull back the slush gates of Heaven

If you walk in these paths, nothing will avert the demonstration and display of My favor toward you.

Jeremiah 6:16   Jeremiah 18:15   Psalm 51:1:14

PERSONAL DISCOVERY

_____
_____
_____

ALL RISE

I entreat you…

Rise higher and higher in your Christian walk. Do not let fleshly attitudes rob you of My intended altitudes. I want you to rise, not just on resurrection morning, but right here today.
I long that you would prove the eagle's…
>Rising power
>Mountain top resting place

Here you have an improved perspective of My plan as I continue to build My church. **Sitting time has passed, soaring time has come**. Your position is not in the depths and debris of this world but in the heights of My glory and splendor.

>**Take your stand**
>**Take your place**

Move up into all the Blood-bought advantages I have afforded you. Eye has not seen or ear heard, nor has it entered into the heart of man what I have prepared for him. Begin now to discard all inhibitions. That which I have vowed I am more than able to perform.

Recollect…Israel sinned, in that they limited the holy One of Israel. That generation failed to enter the promised land because of unbelief.
Beloved…
>**Begin to believe**
>**Start rising toward the top**
>**Lay hold of ever-increasing faith**

My name is El Shaddai, the mighty God, I live in the power of an endless life.

I am the God who called…
  Abraham, from Ur of the Chaldeas, and honored him with the title, 'father of those who walk by faith'

  Joseph, from the pasture, pit and prison and elevated him to the position of nobility and grandeur

  David, from shepherding on the hillside, to become Israel's anointed king and treasured psalmist

My call goes out anew over the valleys and echoes from the mountains…Arise! Arise! Your Master has come and has called for you.

Isaiah 40:31   Psalm 78:41   Genesis 18:14

PERSONAL POSITION

_____
_____
_____

CARRIED AWAY

My people

Some of you are carried away with good churches, good fellowships and even good intentions. The time has come for you to be carried away in a new realm of the Spirit which will enhance the work of My kingdom.

My servant, Ezekiel, was carried away in the Spirit. His assignment was to preach to a dead congregation. He was ready and willing to obey the command and consequently, he and that congregation were revived. Bones lying bleached on the desert sand began coming together by the breath of My Spirit. They stood up as an exceeding great and mighty army.
This scene portrays for the church, three areas of Christian experience...

Restoration
Renewal
Revival

My servant, John, during his exile on the Isle of Patmos, was carried away in the Spirit and was sanctioned to see and hear things which no other has been privileged to witness. His experience was an unveiling revelation. One significant aspect was to reveal a 'carried away' chosen and redeemed people. John caught a glimpse of these martyrs in Heaven and heard a voice behind him saying,

"These are they who have washed their robes and made them white in the Blood of the Lamb."
They are before My throne and serve Me perpetually.

My servant, Philip, the evangelist; was carried away by the Spirit. He was called from the midst of revival blessing in Samaria. By obeying the voice of the Spirit he was extended the opportunity and immense joy of leading the queen's treasurer to saving faith in Me.

Church, the time has come to...
>Cast aside every weight
>Lay up treasure in Heaven
>Love each other as I have loved you

You will be recompensed when you comply with these directives. My blessings upon you will be innumerable and immeasurable, and you too will be...
> **Carried away in the Spirit**

Ezekiel 37:1   Revelation 7:14-17   Hebrews 12:1

>*PERSONAL RESOLVE*

_____
_____
_____

POWER IN PRAISE

I see your dilemma and I am come down to bring you freedom.

My people, I will…
> **Make your bitter water sweet**
> **Make all good things abound toward you**
> **Not leave you deserted in the prison cell**
> **Dispatch My ministering angels who will snap your fetters and set you free**

Raise your hands to Me in praise and adoration
Recall, it was while Moses' hands were lifted high that he and the Israelites triumphed over their enemy

Be not deceived…
Your enemy is very real. The Scriptures affirm he goes about as a roaring lion seeking whom he may devour. His method of attack is to stifle your Christian focus, attempt to denigrate your position in Me and nullify your testimony. He did not retreat after his encounters with Samson, Job and Peter. He is persistently lurking and searching for believers, who like others he can deceive and consume; do not be alarmed, he is a defeated foe. **I am at your side,** and with your armor in place he cannot impair you. Begin now to praise My name…
In praise there is joy, liberty and unending strength.

Jonah gave praise when he was down in the belly

of the great fish

Jehoshaphat gave praise when on his way to battle, led by his singers and musicians

Paul and Silas gave praise when locked in a prison cell, their bleeding feet held fast in stocks.

These veterans of the faith were skilled in...
>Defying the enemy
>Depriving the enemy
>Defeating the enemy

You also can conquer, if you...
>Hold fast to My promises
>Incessantly seek My face in prayer
>Honor My name with wholehearted praise

Live victoriously

Exodus 15:23-25　　*Isaiah 45:2*　　*Acts 16:25*

PERSONAL PRAISE

_____
_____
_____

PROMISES

Many of you are living with problems that can be solved and questions that can be answered.

You have...
>Afflictions that can be removed
>Broken relationships which can be restored

Be strong and of good courage, My hand is outstretched to you, healing virtue is within your reach and in Me all your needs will be supplied.

Windows are opening above you. Doors are opening before you and...
>**Mercy**
>**Forgiveness**
>**Restoration**
>**Refreshment**
>**Fulfilment**

will be yours when you come to Me with humble and contrite hearts.

>**Doubt your doubts**
>**Believe your beliefs**

Step out on My promises...
>A complete and comprehensive pardon for the past
>A beautiful and perfect peace for the present
>A strong and mighty power for living
>A grand and glorious prospect for dying
>A great and blessed place for eternal dwelling

These promises are yea and amen in Me.

Extensive and effectual is the door that is opened to you, it leads to My throne of grace where I unfailingly intercede on your behalf.

Isaiah 52:5   Hebrews 4:16   1 Corinthians 16:19

PERSONAL APPRECIATION

_____
_____
_____

DAY OF DELIVERANCE

My little children

This is your day of dynamic deliverance. As My eye is on the sparrow, so it is fixed on you. Constantly I watch over you and observe your oppression, bondage and pain. I am here to set you free.

I see you walking the valley of...
>Guilt and shame
>Turmoil and frustration
>Failure and fear

I see your vulnerability as you trudge the road of wounds, grievances and afflictions, effectuated by those who were once friends. This hurt has become entrenched in your spirit and that which was once a molehill has now become a mountain.
If you...
>Cry out to Me
>Walk before Me and obey My voice

I will remove those offensive mountains
See you through those burdensome valleys
Lift you up from every dungeon and set your feet on high places

It is written...
>**If the Son shall set you free, you shall be free indeed**

Freedom is your Blood-bought legacy, purchased at the cross of Calvary.

The apostle Paul said, "O wretched man that I am,

who shall deliver me from this body of death? Who can set me free?" He articulated, "**I thank God, through Jesus Christ our Lord.**" He immediately offered up to Me the sacrifice of praise and thanksgiving.

Dear ones, this is the acceptable year of the Lord, the day of jubilee.
    I love you, and you are free to go

John 8:36   1 Corinthians 13:6   Romans 7:24

PERSONAL ACCEPTANCE

_____
_____
_____

THIS MOUNTAIN

I announced to My servant Moses, "You have been at this mountain long enough." At this time the children of Israel were in a state of apathy and little was being accomplished in My name. The promise of Canaan made to them in earlier times was not fulfilled because of unbelief.

The call goes out again...
>> You have stayed at this mountain long enough
>> Prepare to advance
>> You are going on and going through

My people! There are other...
>> **Mountains to climb**
>> **Battles to be won**
>> **Possessions to be possessed**

No man-made barricades will keep My people out. Canaan is yours 'for the taking.'

Press ahead...
>> Pull up your stakes
>> Take down your tents
>> Stretch out your curtains
>> Lengthen your cords

I am ready to expand your influence and increase your borders.

I have set before you a land...
>> **Of promise and fulfilment**
>> **Fruitfulness and plenty**
>> **Flowing with milk and honey**

Let not the inhabitants harass you. As I was with Moses, so shall I be with you. Those who appear to you as giants, are as grasshoppers in My sight.

Be joyful...
   I, who brought you out of Egypt, will undoubtedly bring you into Canaan.

One with Me is greater than all of them

Deuteronomy 1:6   Obadiah 1:17   Psalm 119:106

PERSONAL PROGRESS

_____
_____
_____

THE RIVER IS FLOWING

My covenant people

In My dwelling place a river is flowing, from which all your needs can be supplied. Full provision has been made for every man.

> There is forgiveness for sin
> Freedom from bondage
> Redemption for hungry and hurting hearts

For you who have come to this river…
I called, chose and clothed you
I anointed you and set you aside to publish My name among the nations
I placed the dew of My Spirit upon you to flow down over you to the soles of your feet. Here I command My blessing, even life for evermore

To enter this new domain and move into the river, it is imperative to say farewell to all forms of personal reputation.
> Follow after godliness
> Flee all appearance of evil
> Fight the good fight of faith

Let it never be said, you sat down by the riverside after hanging your harps on the willows.

You are My special treasure. Begin now with renewed determination to lift up My name in the sanctuary.

Lift up your hands in My name
Stand up and bless Me

My river is full and sweeping freely toward you. When you move out into its uninterrupted ever-rolling waters, My holy Spirit will cause other rivers to flow out from you, resulting in blessing and praise to My name.

Psalm 46:4   Revelation 22:1-2   Psalm 133

PERSONAL PARTICIPATION

_____
_____
_____

YES, LORD

A fresh wind of the Holy Spirit is blowing across the land, and speaking potently to the churches, with reference to…
Prophecy, and the priesthood of all believers

Are you seriously seeking to be a blessing with the gift My Spirit has entrusted to you?
Do you desire to increase your ability to hear from Me?
Do you contemplate…
> Operating in the arena of the miraculous?
> Inspiring, and edifying the flock?
> Giving wisdom and direction to those who are perplexed or have been diverted from the truth?

Are you prepared to accept My word and conform to My will? Are you willing to be found in the place of loneliness, rejection and misunderstanding, being answerable only to Me? Can you adjust to being ostracized, your zeal being stifled and your reputation placed on the line? Are you ready to be left bruised and bleeding on the sideline, carrying 'ministry scars' for years to come? If your answer is, "Yes! Yes Lord, I am willing and ready." Then…
> **Open your heart**
> **Step out in faith**
> **Come! Follow Me to the upper room**

The 'upper room' represents My Holy Spirit descending on the disciples as a mighty rushing wind.

Here He filled...
All the house
All the disciples
All Jerusalem
Now He is filling the world.
On that day much joy and blessing were exhibited in every street as the Divine word was proclaimed, prophecy fulfilled and three thousand people were saved. Some of the crowd mocked and said, "These men are full of new wine." The truth is; they were full of the Spirit's New Wine, as prophesied in the book of Joel...On that day the mountains will drip with new wine...as My Spirit is poured out on all flesh.

Entering and moving freely in this 'new wine' experience will equip you for your vocation. It will enable you to exercise your spiritual gifts within **My royal priesthood.**

Blessed are you who hunger and thirst...you too shall be filled

Acts 1:4-5   *Acts 2:17*   *Joel 3:18*

PERSONAL CALLING

_____
_____
_____

MY HOUSE

It shall be in the last days that **My House will be established throughout the land** and the gates of hell shall not prevail against it. It shall be exalted above all others; the nations of the world will run into it.

Many shall say, "Come and let us go up to the house of the Lord, there His...
> **Word is expounded**
> **Way is explained**
> **Will is expressed.**"

It is a place of paramount importance for those who have been brought out of darkness into My marvelous light. It has been devised, dedicated and identified throughout the Scriptures as a...

House of praise... David writes, "The precepts and statutes of the Lord I will sing within His house."

House of prayer... This was a statute established when the church was in critical disarray.

House of provision...The prophet Malachi said, "Bring all the tithes into the storehouse...that there may be food in My house."

Let not the words I uttered in the days of My flesh be repeated today, "O Jerusalem, Jerusalem, how often would I have gathered you under My wing, but you would not...See, your house is left desolate... That which was ordained to be a place of prayer, you have turned into a den of thieves."

It is apparent that there are two satanic forces impacting My house today; controversy and disunity. Both echo the church's current spiritual condition. This has resulted in sin in the camp and a lack of passion and purpose among My people. My house being characterized as a...
> Well without water
> Tree without fruit
> Lamp without oil

Revealing only emptiness, lifelessness and powerlessness.

Beloved, it is high time to return to the old paths and begin digging the old wells. It is not too late to make an 'about turn' and start again. You can still reiterate the words of My servant, "I would rather be a doorkeeper in the house of the Lord, than dwell in the tents of the wicked...A day in His house is better than a thousand in the courts of unbelievers."

Malachi 3:10   Mark 11:17   Psalm 84:10

PERSONAL RESTORATION

_____
_____
_____

SPIRITUAL WARFARE

The devil is on the warpath...

His objective is to bring down and overthrow Christian witness and activity in the world. Since the beginning of time he has been devising ways whereby he can render the church ineffective, but this can never happen. There has always been and always will be a nucleus of people who are willing and prepared to love, follow and serve Me at any cost.

Because I love My church and gave Myself for it, I will not suffer the enemy to usurp or obstruct My final purposes for it. Reflect; concerning the devil and his deceptions...I have been violent toward him and I require My church to do the same. From the days of John the Baptist the church has suffered violence and the violent take it by force. My people shall not be outwitted, neither shall they be put to shame. I have laid the foundation. I am the Chief Cornerstone and committed to seeing the final stone laid. For Zion's sake I will not keep silent until her righteousness shines out as the dawn.

By the efficacy of My Blood and the mention of My name you can and will overcome

My ministry involves...
                       Pulling down
                       Casting out
           Overthrowing the works of the enemy

Children, go and do likewise. Preach the Gospel... Cast out demons...Speak with new tongues...Lay hands on the sick and they shall recover.

Spiritual warfare continues in the heavens and on earth, the devil being the chief instigator. But fear not, you are called and equipped to...
          Wage war against the enemy
                    Triumph
          Be more than conquerors
through the presence and function of the Holy Spirit within you.

From before the foundation of the world, I determined that you should be...
              Winners and not losers
                Heads and not tails
                Above and not below

Lift up your banners and shout for joy, for I am mighty in valor and strong in battle.

Raise your eyes to the hills, see Me, and the armies of Heaven...
            Shields are presented
  Swords are wielded and shining bright
Shouts of victory rise up within the camp
      The battle cry has been sounded
            We are 'at the ready'
         The enemy will be defeated

Mark 16:17-18   Deut. 1:8   11 Chronicles 20:15

Streams Of Sonlight

PERSONAL PLEDGE

_____
_____
_____

YOUR WORD

IS A LAMP TO MY FEET

AND

A LIGHT TO MY PATH

Psalm 119:105

HOMECOMING

Beloved

Because of My supreme sacrifice on Calvary, and since you have accepted Me as Lord of your life, your past is pardoned and your future secure. Through faith, you have everlasting peace through the **Blood of the New Covenant**

When you reach your eternal home, which is prepared as a bride adorned for her husband, you will be endowed with many blessings and the greatest of these will be...
Your final transformation

Your work will be done.
You will be complete in Me.

You will...
Hear the words I speak
Wear a crown of faithfulness
Walk on streets paved with gold

Your feet will dance at the sound of My name and your eyes behold the wonder of...
My grace and glory

No longer will you see Me as through a glass, darkly. Face to face you will stand before Me, and see Me as I am.

You will meet...

Patriarchs
Prophets
Priests

and faithful, honorable saints of the early church, every member of the household of faith and loved ones who have already come home.

You will bow in My presence and extol Me...**Savior, Lord and King**

Church! Prepare for a great **Homecoming**

Colossians 1:20-22   Rev. 21:1-5   Colossians 2:10

PERSONAL PREPARATION

_____
_____
_____

WORTHY IS THE LAMB

I call upon you...
   Sing to Me with psalms, hymns and spiritual songs
     Worship Me in the beauty of holiness
       Bow down and give Me glory
Let the...
Heavens rejoice
Earth be glad
Trees of the field clap their hands
Mountains and hills show forth their praise

Give thanks to Me for I am good, My love and mercy endures for ever
Proclaim My salvation from day to day
Declare My glory to the people
Tell of My marvelous works among the sons of men

I, the Lord your God, omnipotent reigns...
I am high and lifted up
Mine is the kingdom, the power and the glory
I am exalted far above all

Let the church militant join with the church triumphant as they sing...
"Worthy is the Lamb who was slain
He has redeemed us to God
Has made us partakers of His divine nature
By the Blood of the cross, He has given us the victory
He is worthy, for He has created all things and without Him they would cease to exist. He is the...
One who was

Who is
And who is to come
Alpha and Omega...Beginning and the End

Let us kneel before Him and give Him praise."

1 Chronicles 16:8-36   Isaiah 55:12   Rev. 4:8-14

PERSONAL PRAISE AND WORSHIP

_____
_____
_____

YOUR KING COMES

This is Jesus the King. These words were written above My Son's head when He died on Calvary's cross. He is acclaimed as...
>   **King of kings and Lord of lords**

He is no longer the lowly Jesus who rode humbly into Jerusalem sitting on a colt, the foal of a donkey. He is the One John saw coming down out of Heaven on a white horse, accompanied by Heaven's armies, clothed in fine white linen and riding white horses. On His head were many crowns. On His robe and thigh were written the words...
>   **King of kings and Lord of lords**

The word went forth from Heaven, praise the Lord all you...
>   **His saints**
>   **Who fear His name**
>   **Who look for His appearing**

Be glad...
>   He is coming and will not tarry
>   He is not slack concerning His promise

He is coming...
>   **Personally**
>   **Powerfully**
>   **Purposefully**
>   **...to catch the church away**

Hear the hooves of heavenly horses
See the awesome sight in the sky

Smell the fragrance of His presence

Let all the mountains, all the great seas and all of creation cry out, "Alleluia, our redemption is at hand."

Volumes of praise rise up from the priesthood of all believers, as they unite to sing…"Holy, holy, holy, Lord God almighty, the whole earth is full of Your glory.

> By Your power You created all things
> By Your wisdom, set lights in the sky
> By Your Blood You redeemed us

Your works praise You. Your saints praise You Kings of the earth lay their crowns at Your feet."

Isaiah 6:1   Revelation 19:11   Revelation 5:6-7

PERSONAL ANTICIPATION

_____
_____
_____

I AM

I am the great **I Am,** and greatly to be praised.

Who do men say that I am? To the...
**Shepherd...I am the Passover Lamb
Baker...I am the Bread of Life
Thirsty...I am the Water of Life
Sick...I am the Great Physician
Sorrowing...I am the Oil and the Wine
Archaeologist...I am the Rock of Ages
Astronomer...I am the Bright and Morning Star
Architect...I am the Chief Cornerstone**

I am the...
**Fountain that was opened for sin and all uncleanness
Rose of Sharon and the Lily of the Valley
Fourth Man in the burning, fiery furnace
Friend that sticks closer than a brother
Owner of cattle on a thousand hills
Author and Finisher of your faith**

I am not willing that any should perish, but that all should come to repentance.

Psalm 145:1   *2 Peter 3:9*   *Psalm 150:6*

PERSONAL DECLARATION

_____
_____

IF YOU ABIDE IN ME

AND

MY WORDS ABIDE IN YOU

YOU WILL ASK WHAT

YOU DESIRE

AND IT SHALL BE DONE

FOR YOU

JOHN 15:7